ISBN-13:978-1542821247
ISBN-10:154282124X

The Tasteful Letter T

Coloring Book

By Peggy Louise Parrish

C. 2017

Welcome to the world of Letter T.

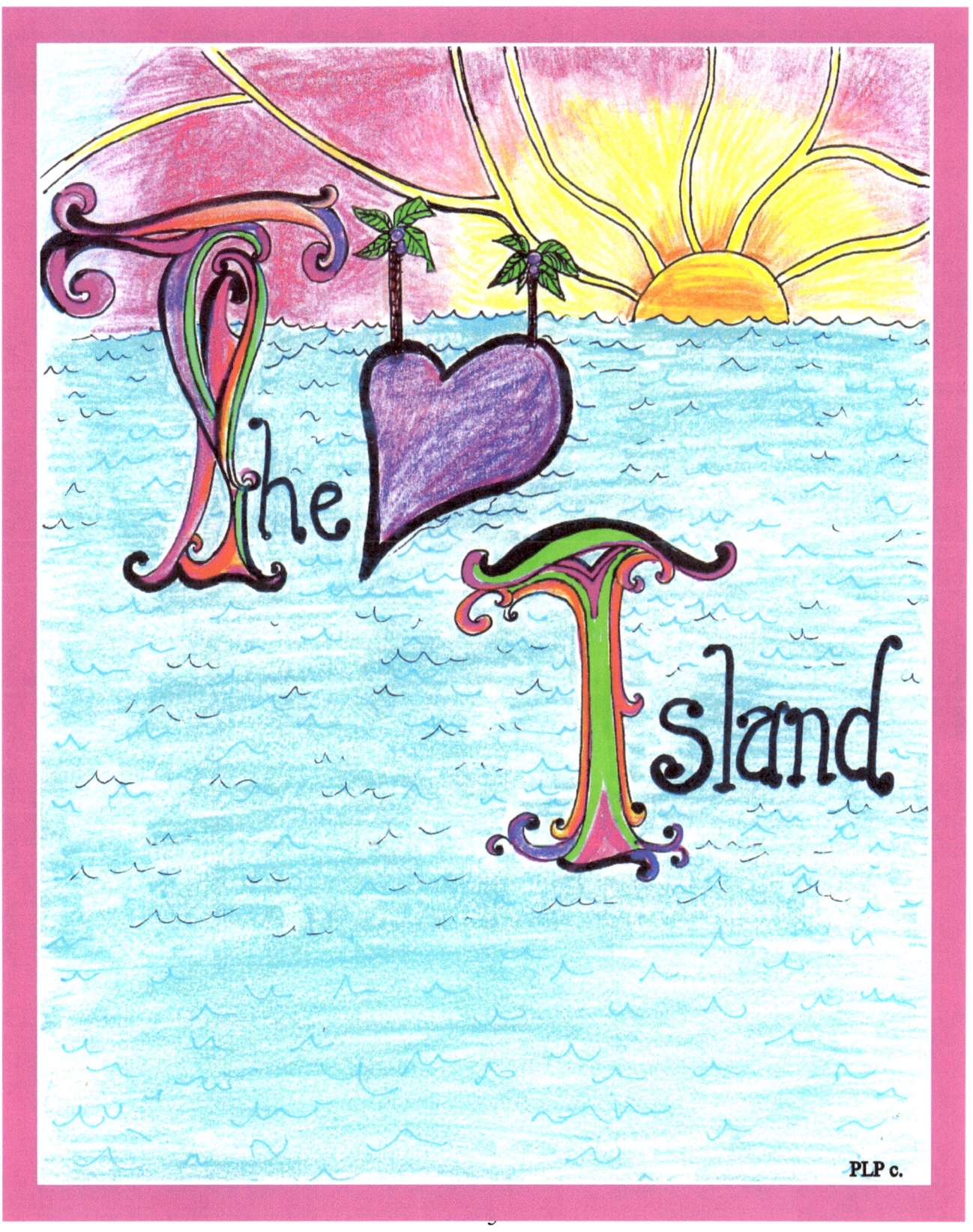

How does the letter T look with wallpaper drawn behind it?

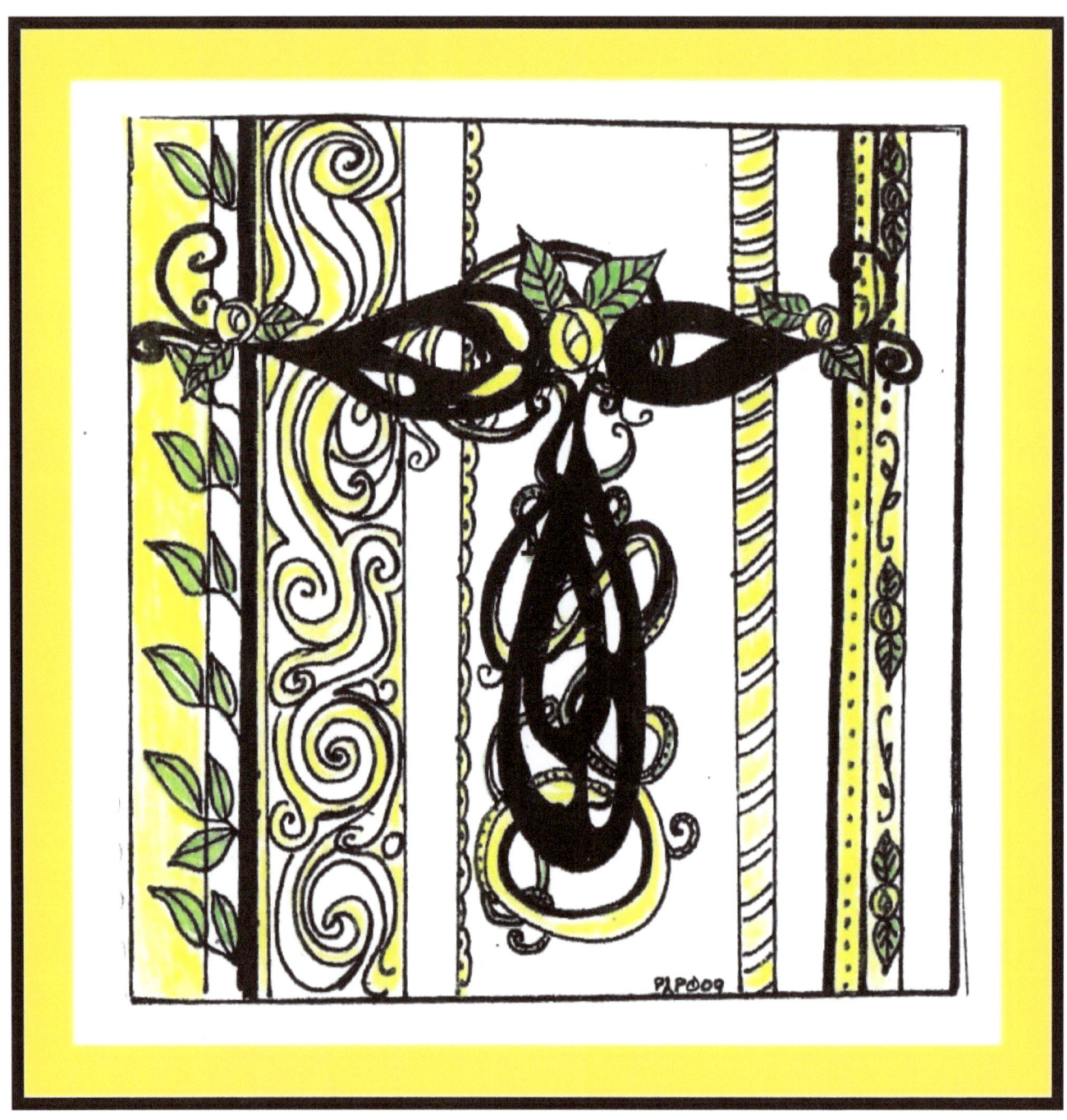

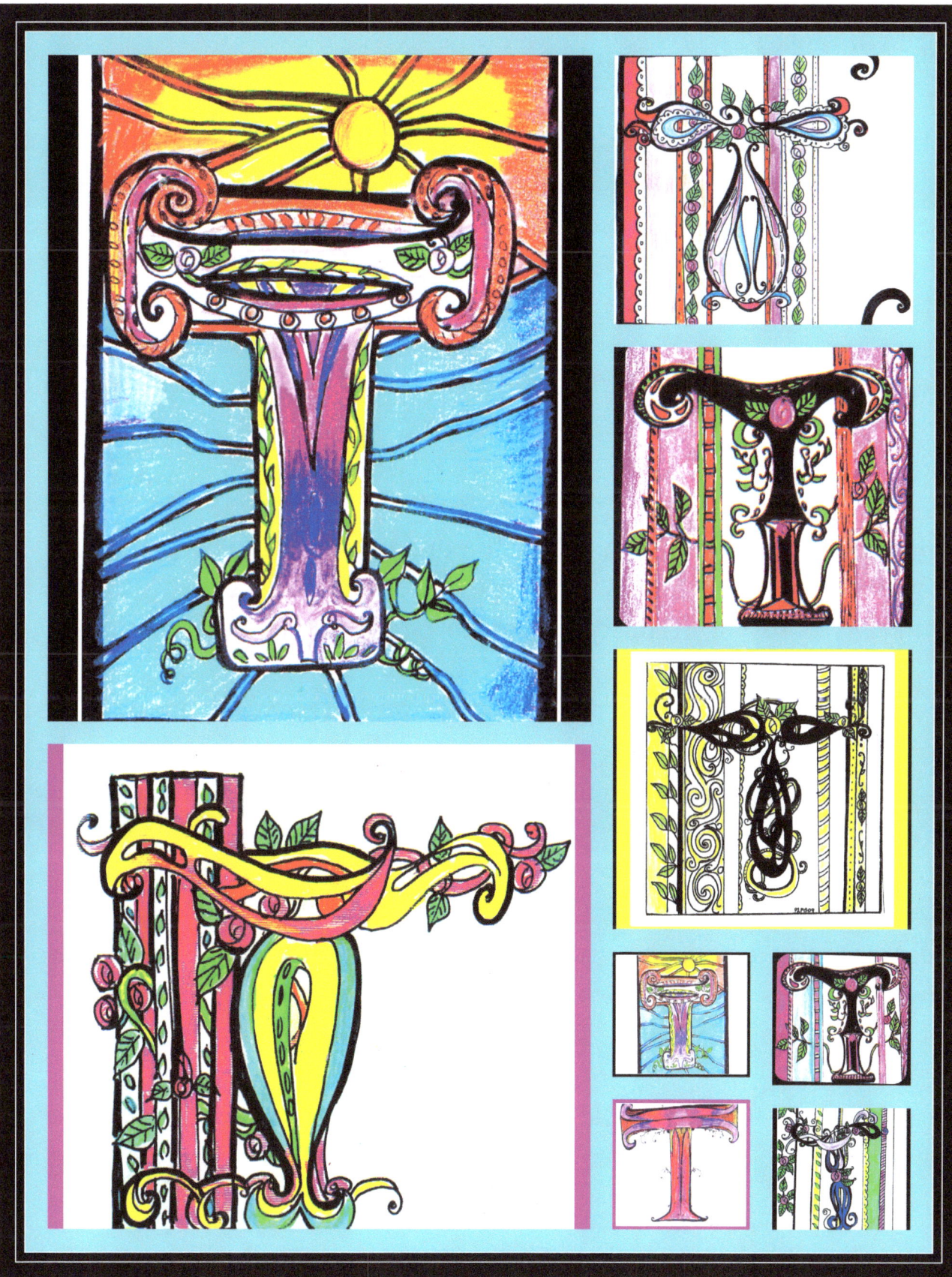

Now it's time for you to have some Coloring Fun. Maybe you have a first or last name that begins with a T. The letter T can send quite a message at the beginning of a word. You may choose how you want to color the T letters in this book. You can copy some of the color ideas that are showed as examples. Or if you want to color them completely different go ahead and have fun.

Quality colored pencils are one of the preferred ways to color these. However you may want to try watercolor pencils, markers or paint. If so, be sure to place a scrap piece of paper behind the page you are coloring till you are done. You may make a few "in house" copies of any letters you want to try in different colors. Keep the PLP initials that are on each page. Feel free to make a print or two of your work for a card or gift. (Please do not sell anything you make from these letters.) Hopefully you will find these pages so much fun that you will want to make up your own letter Ts. Enjoy!

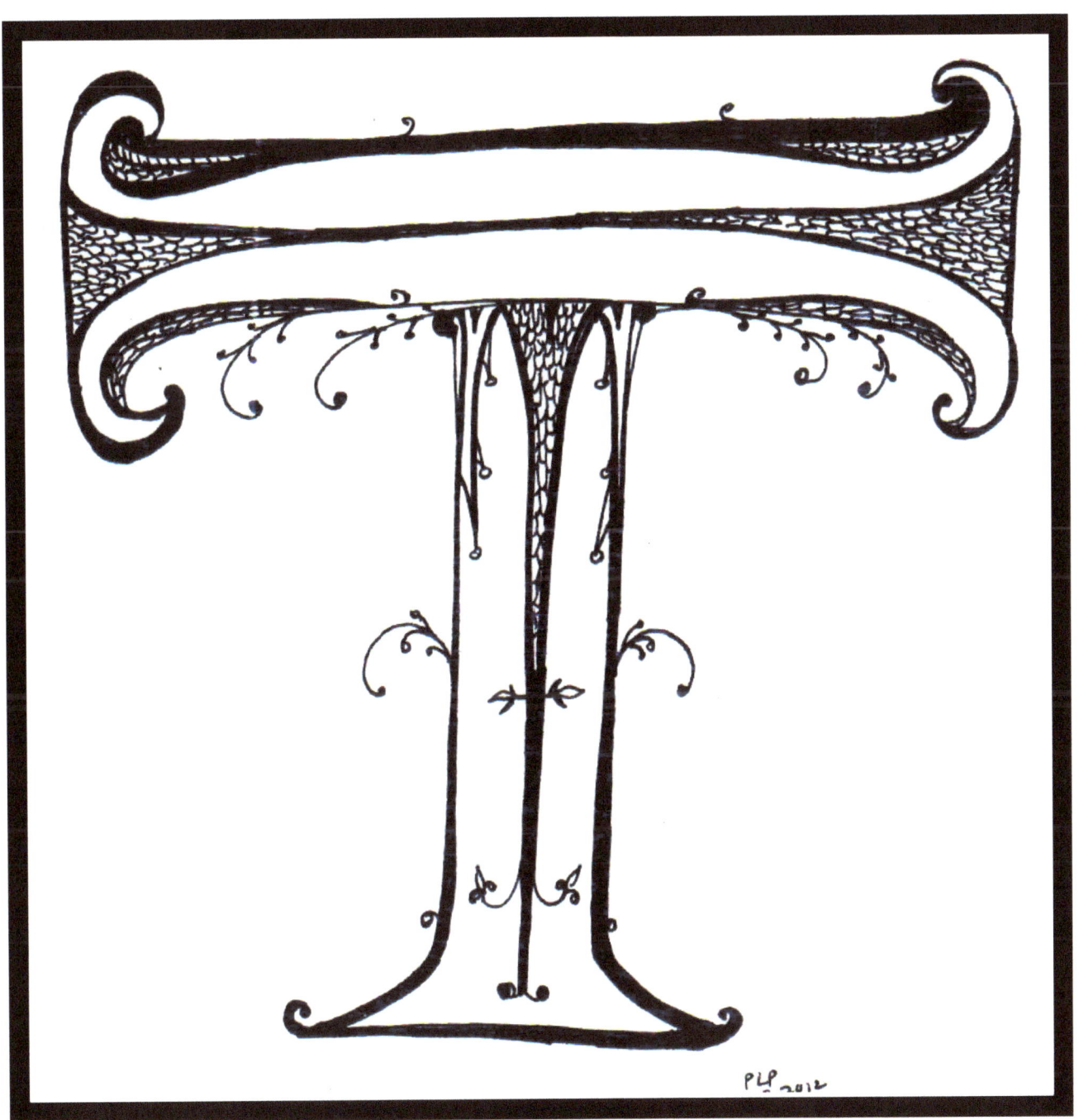

PLP 2012

9

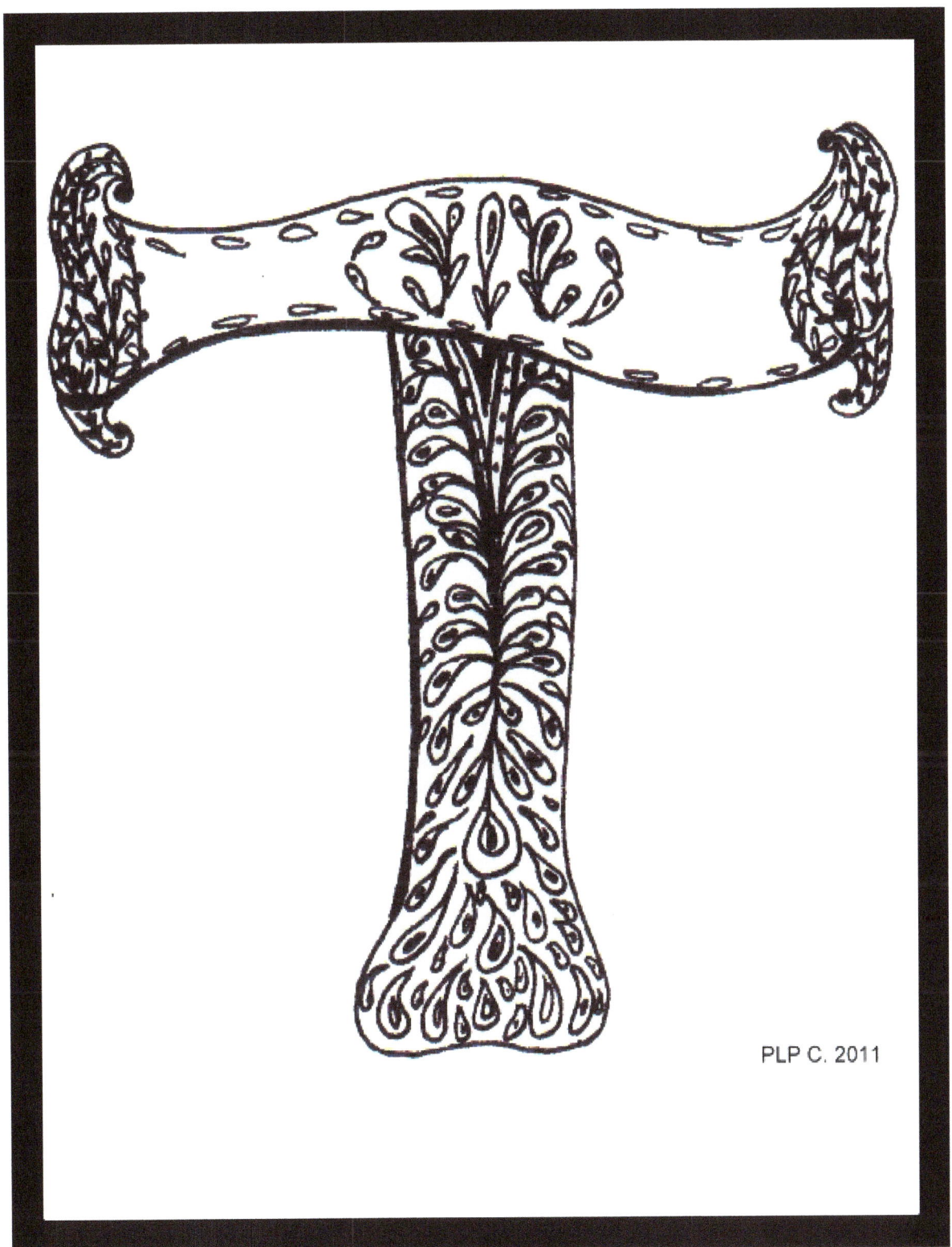

PLP C. 2011

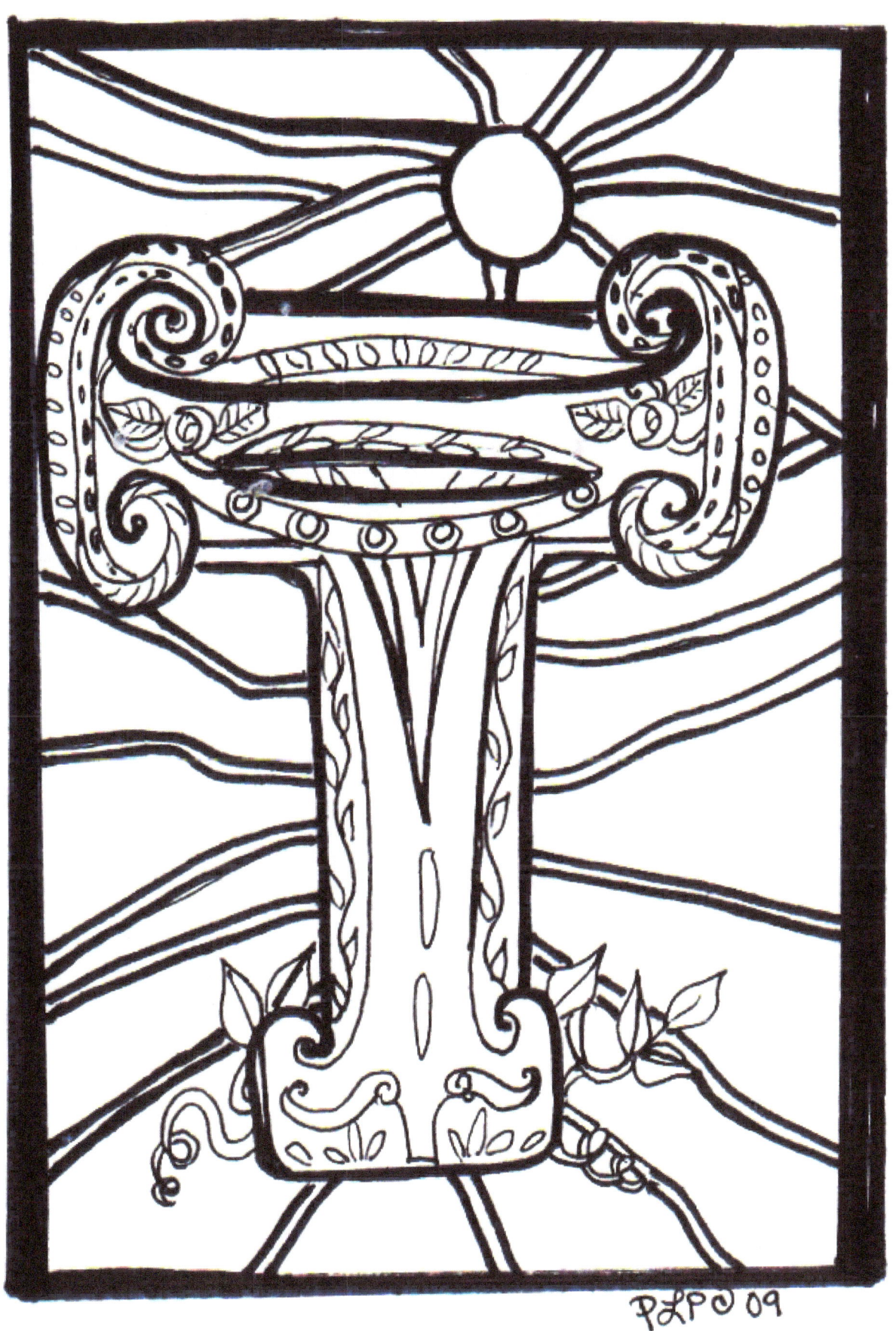

15

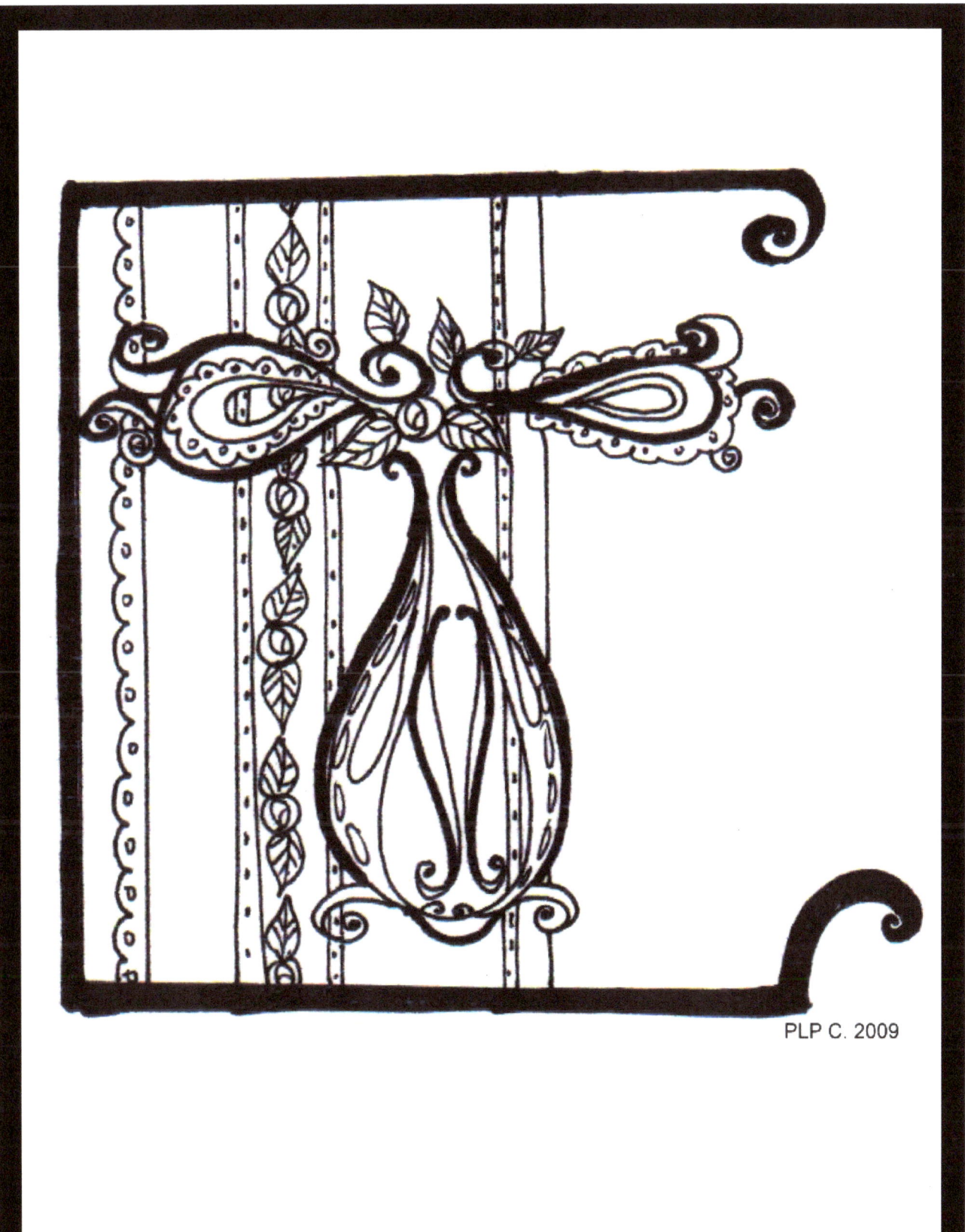

PLP C. 2009

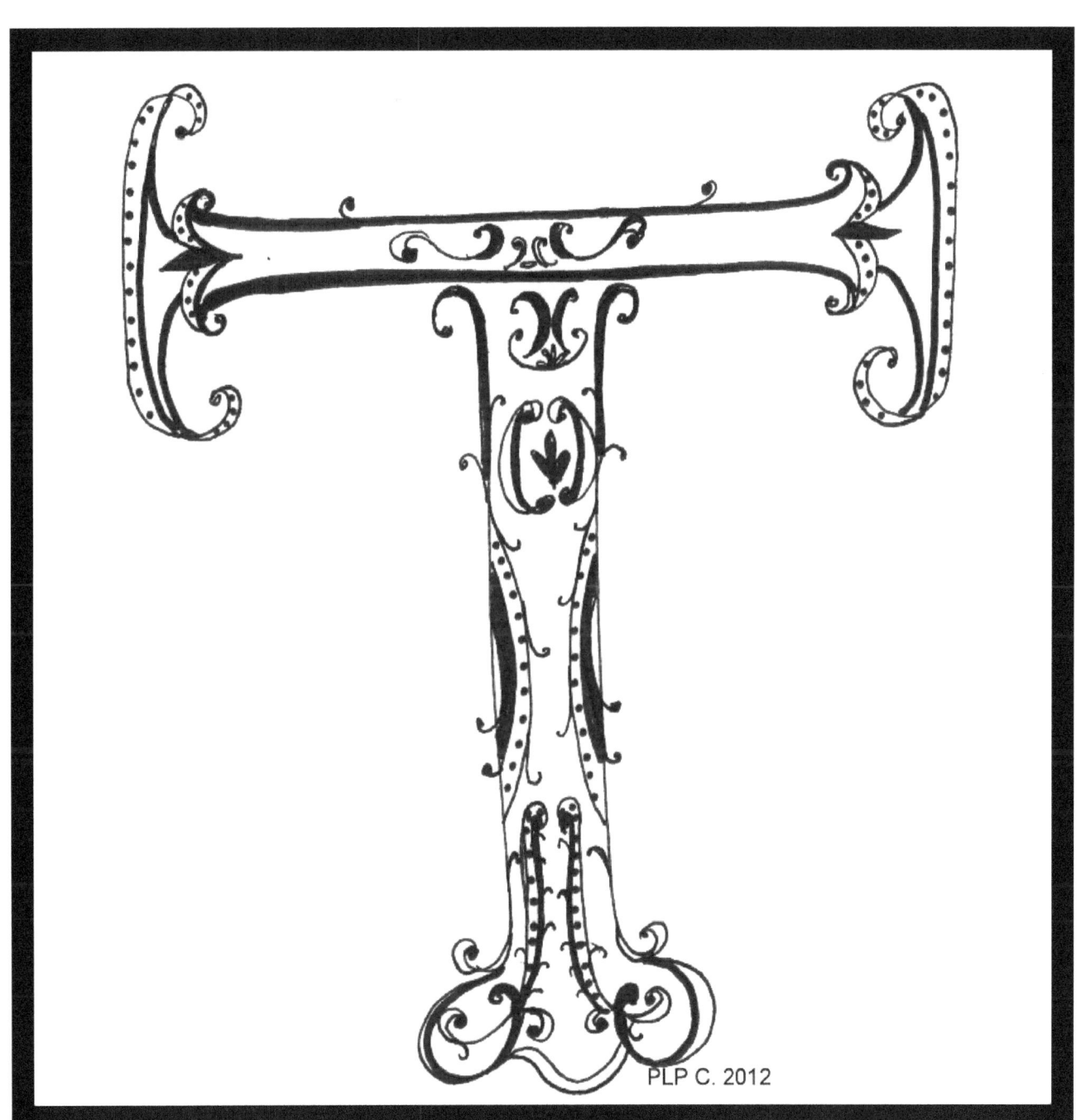

PLP C. 2012

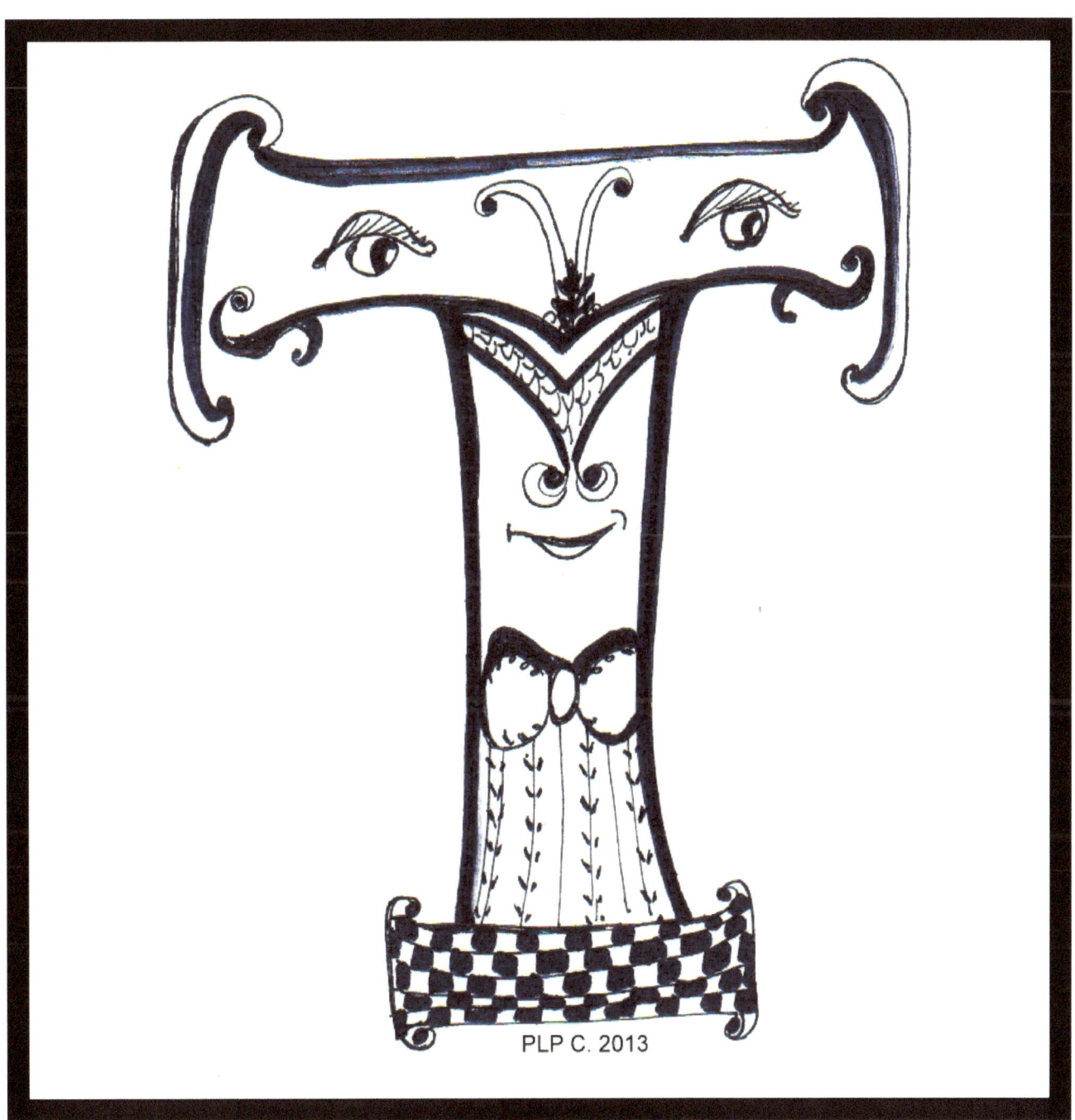

PLP C. 2013

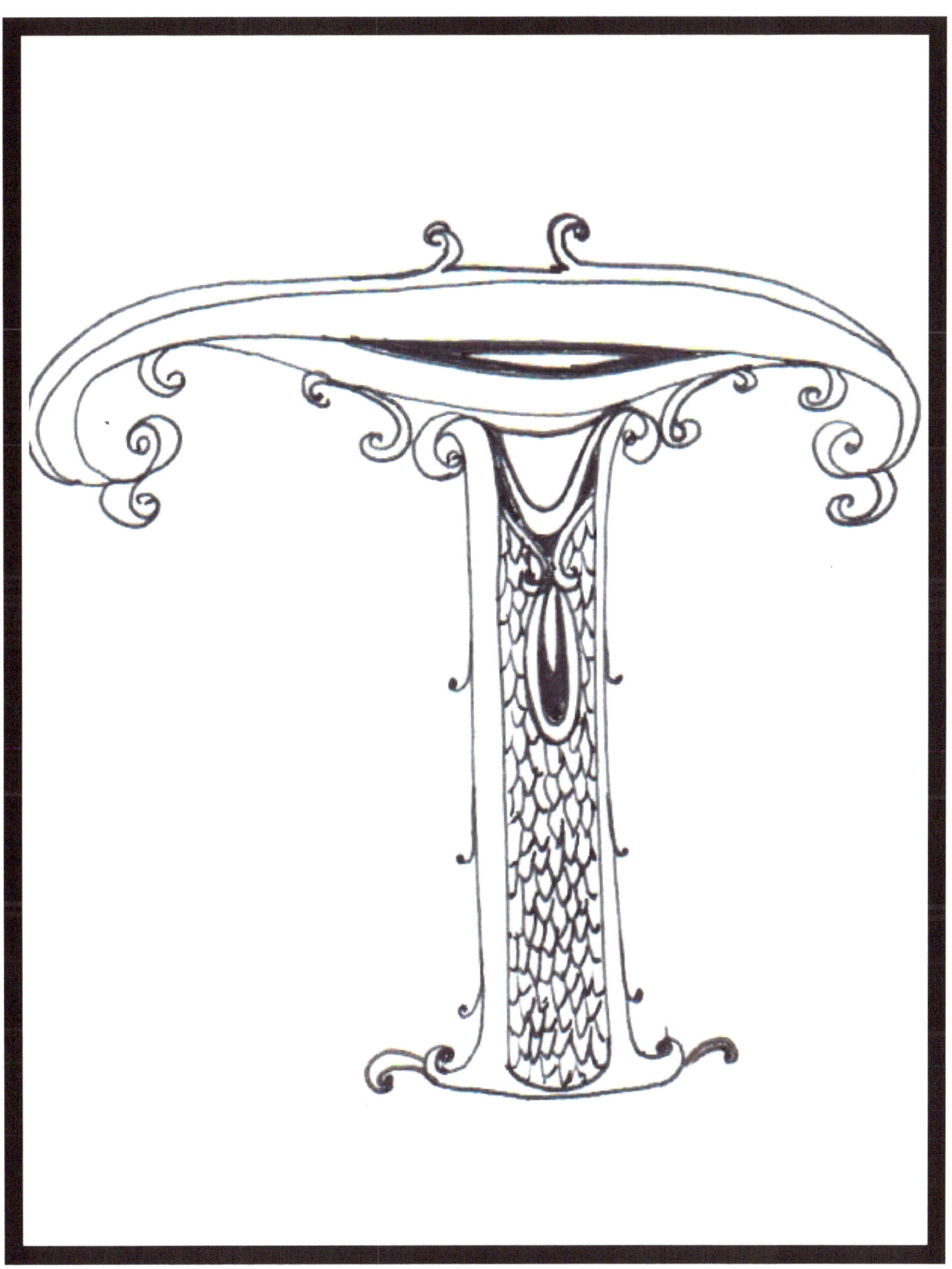

23

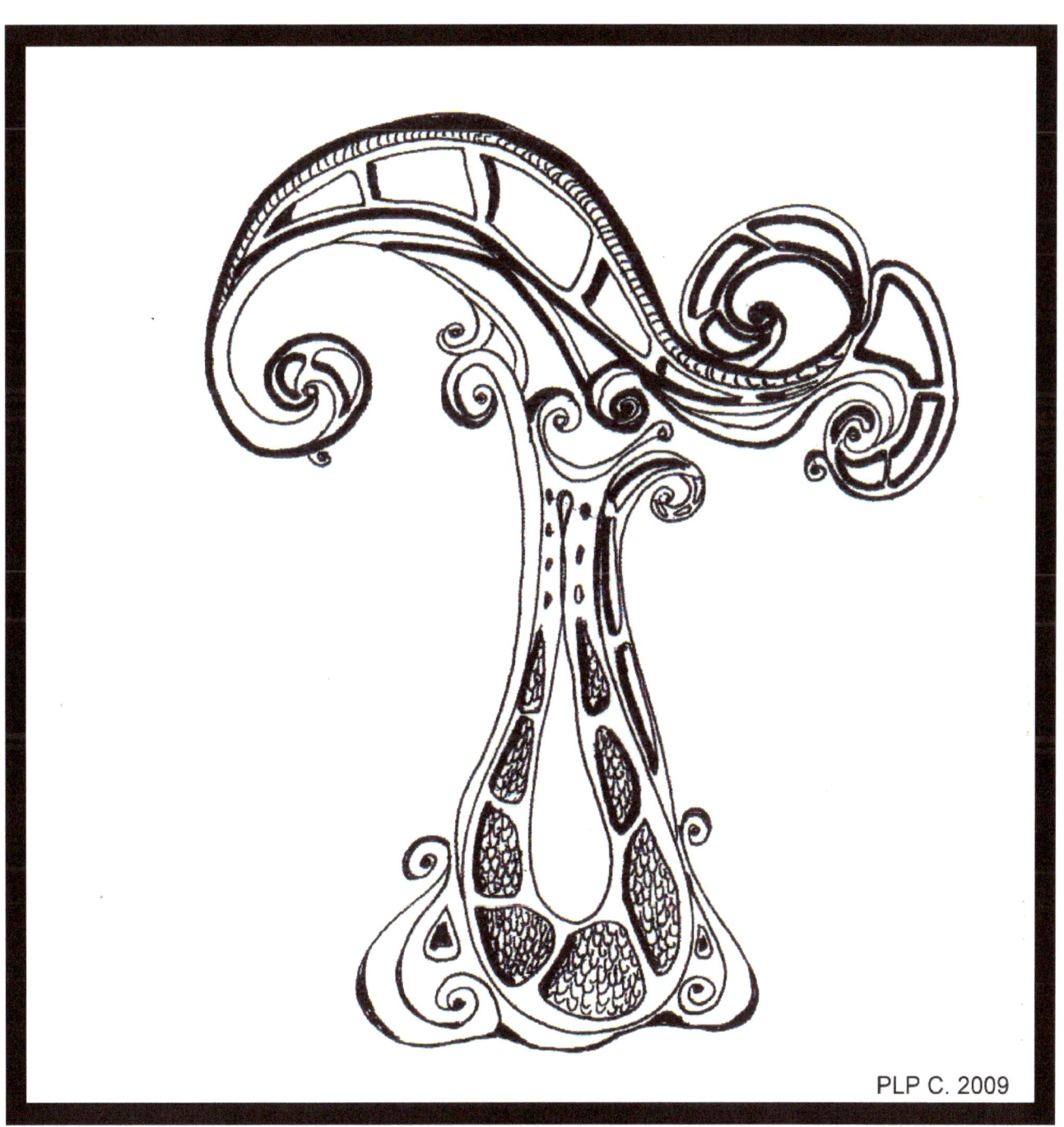

PLP C. 2009

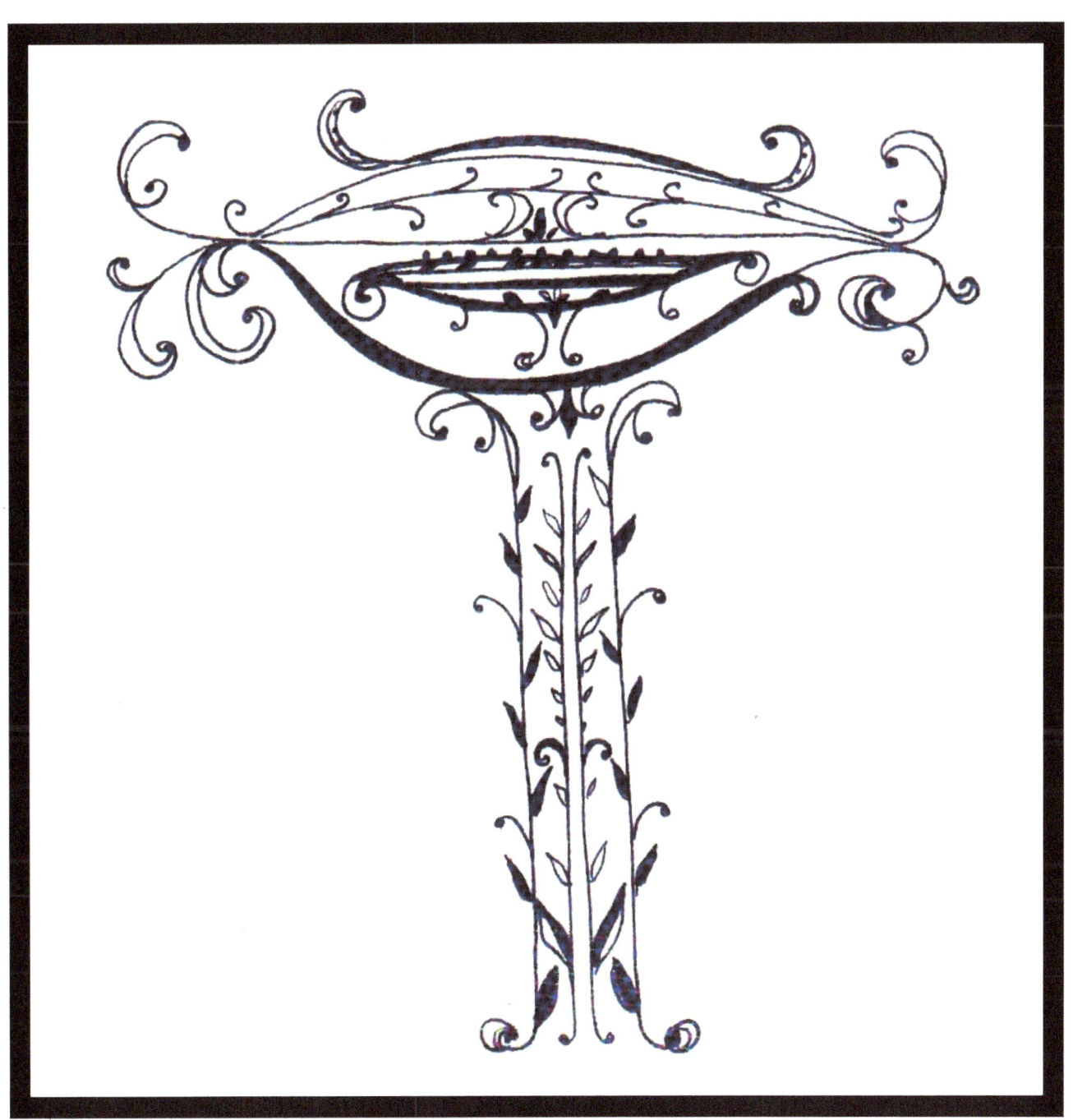

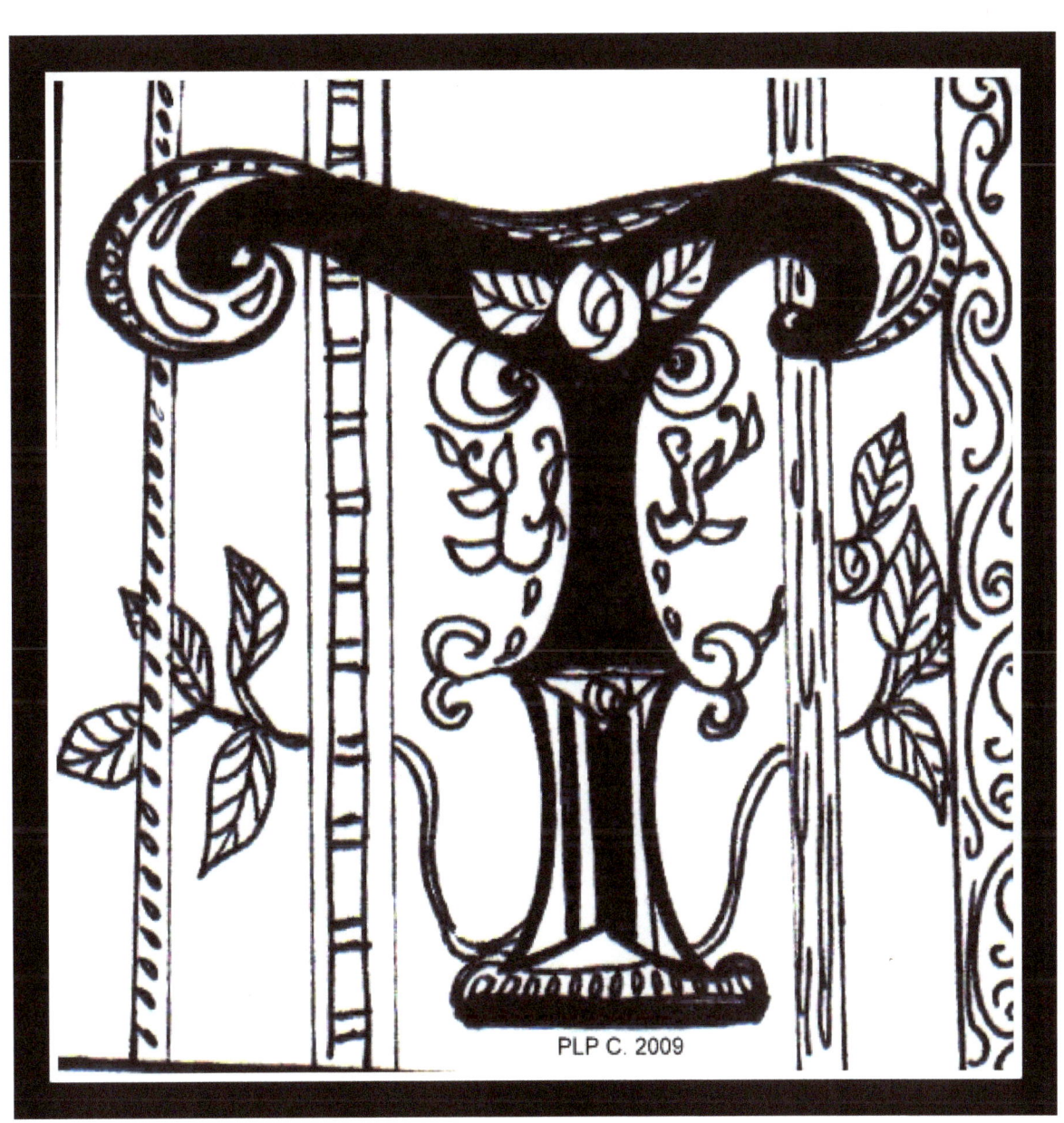

PLP C. 2009

PLP C. 2013

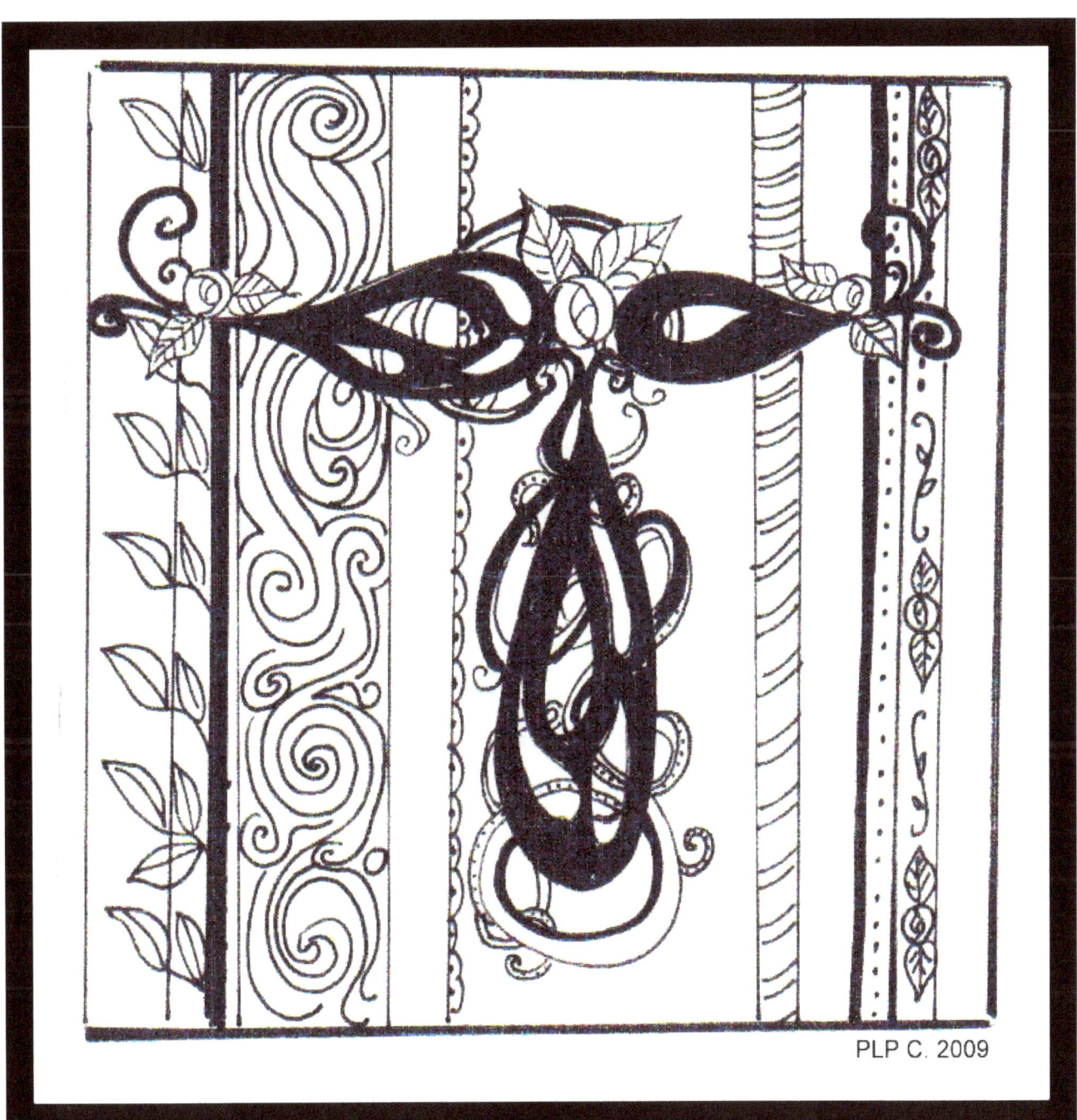

PLP C. 2009

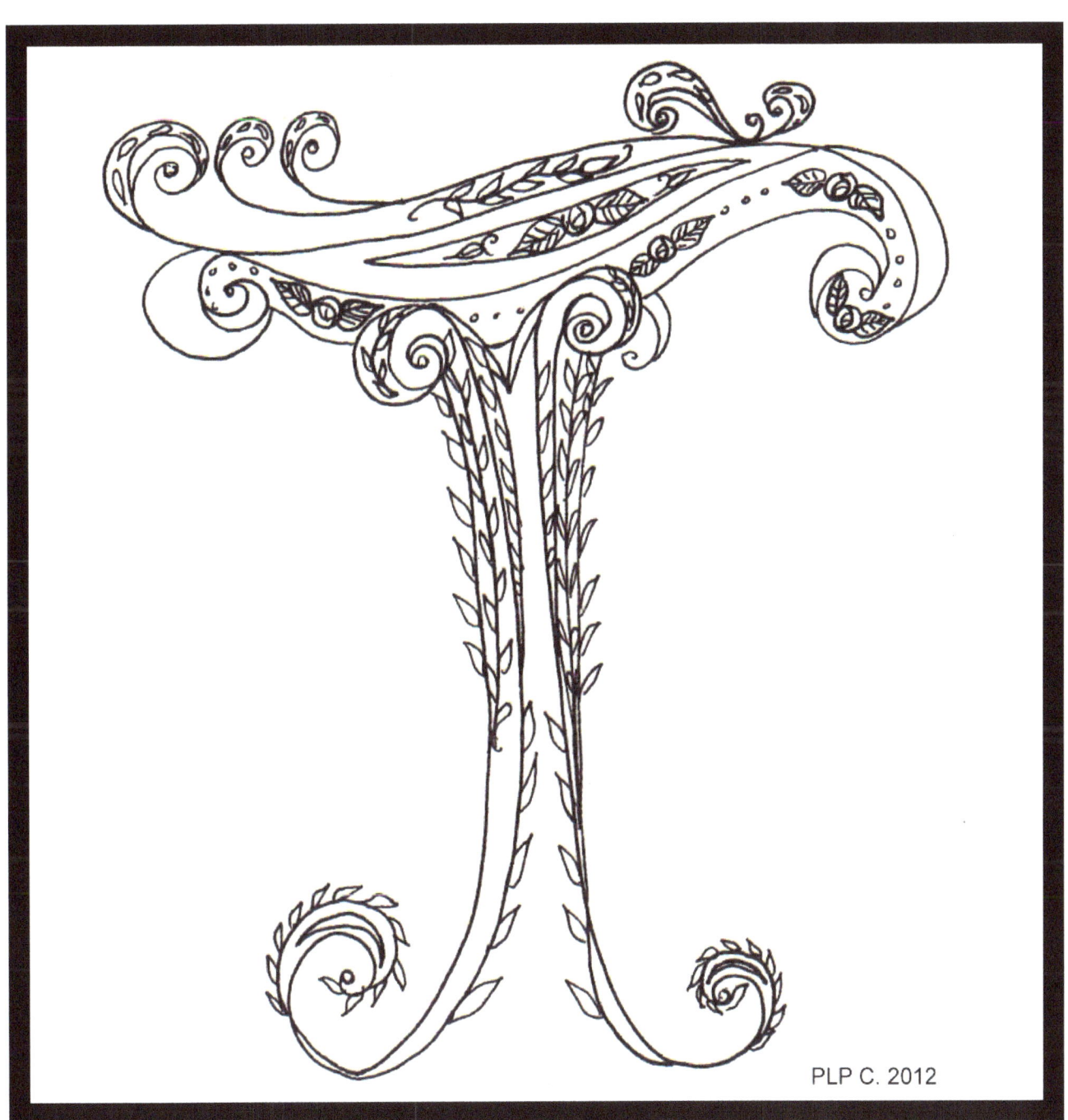

PLP C. 2012

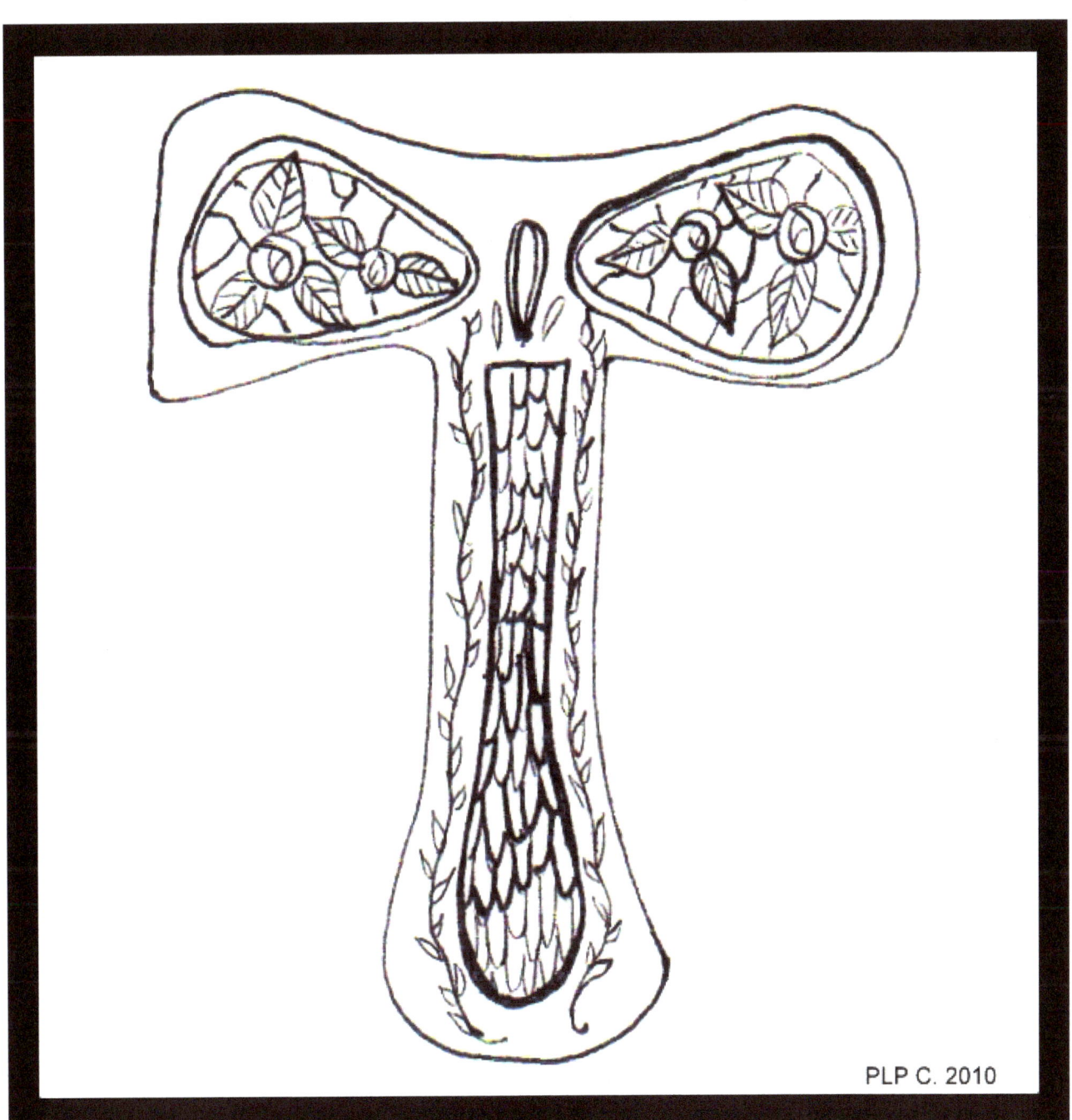

PLP C. 2010

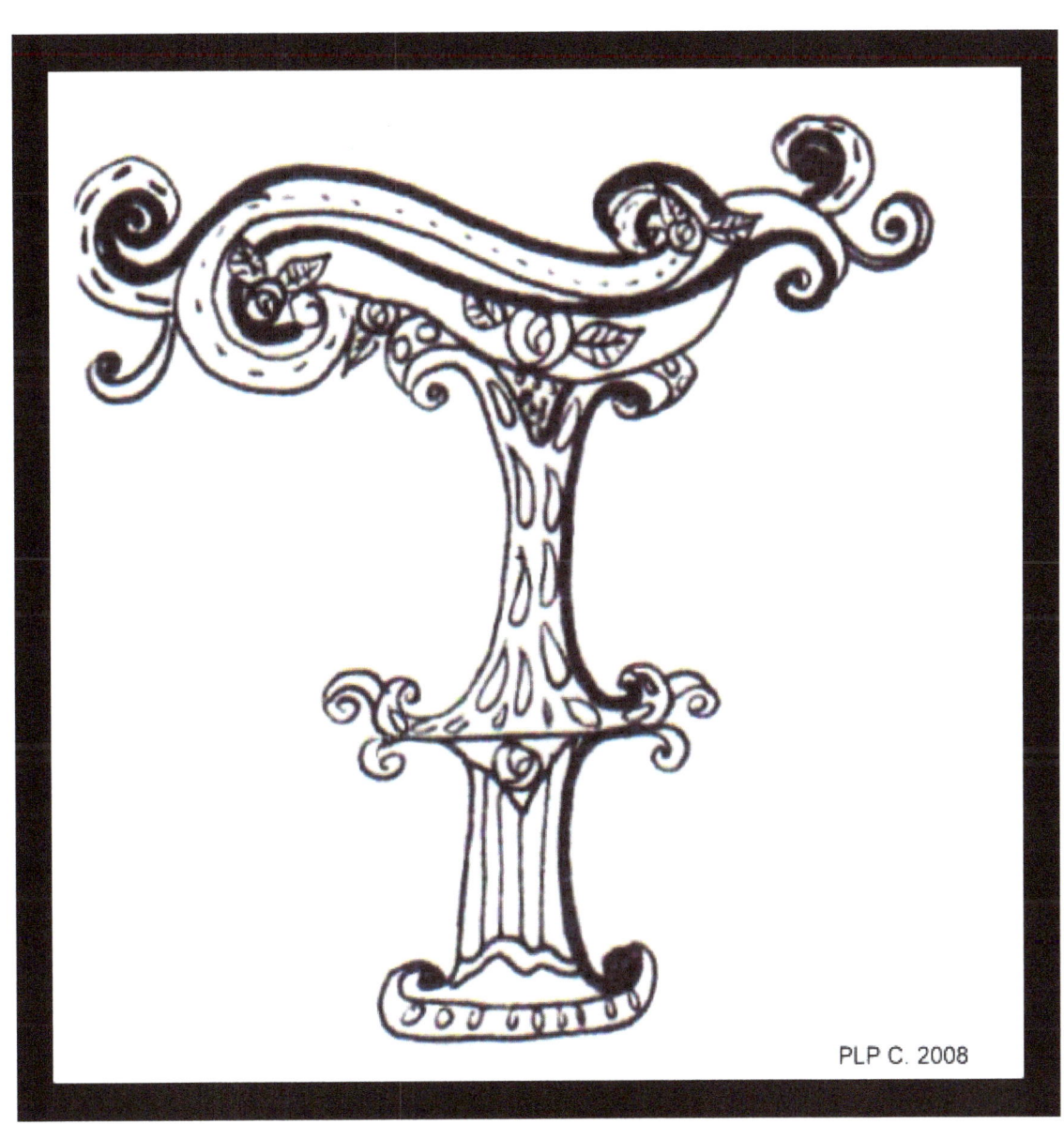

PLP C. 2008

39

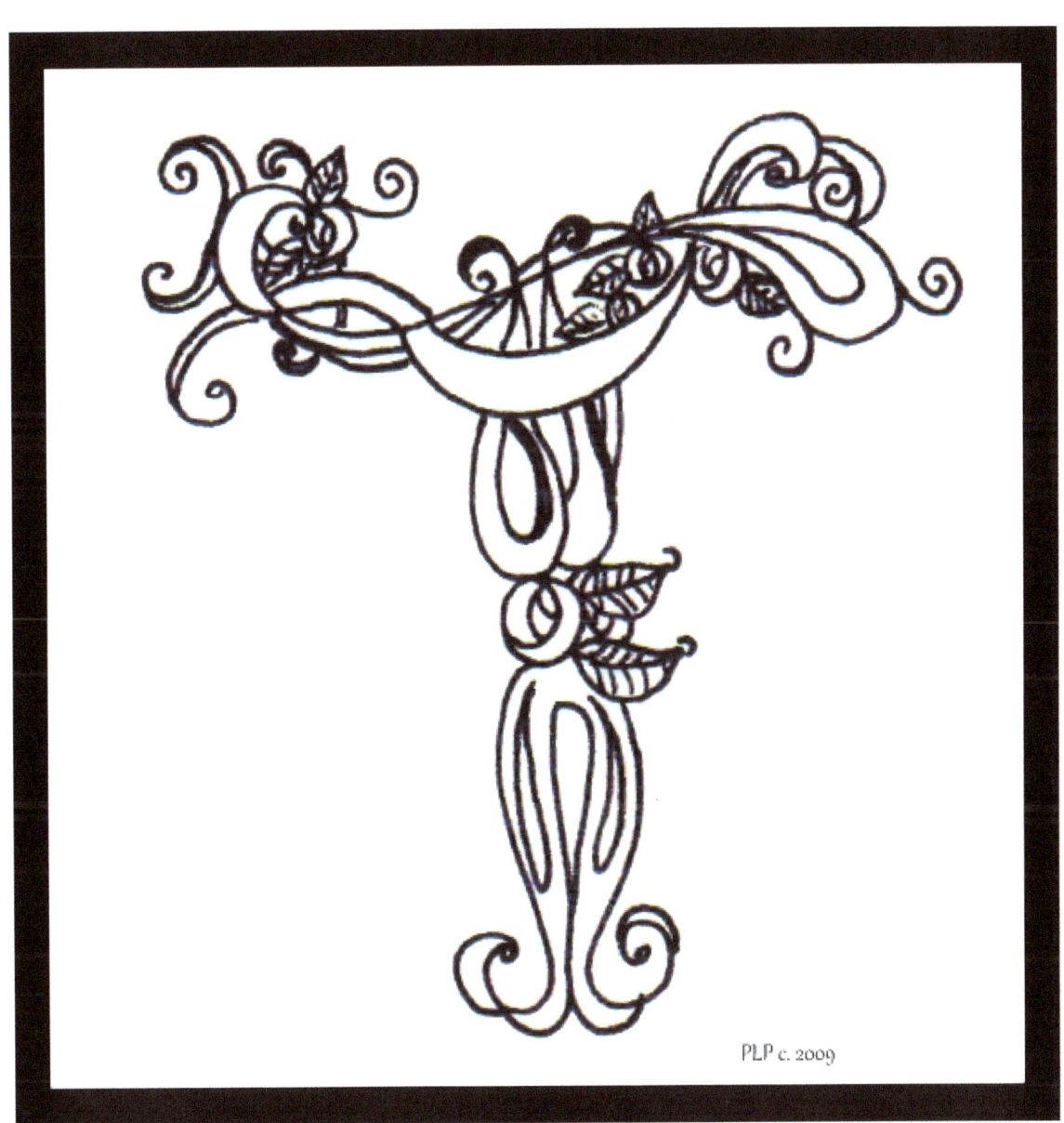

PLP c. 2009

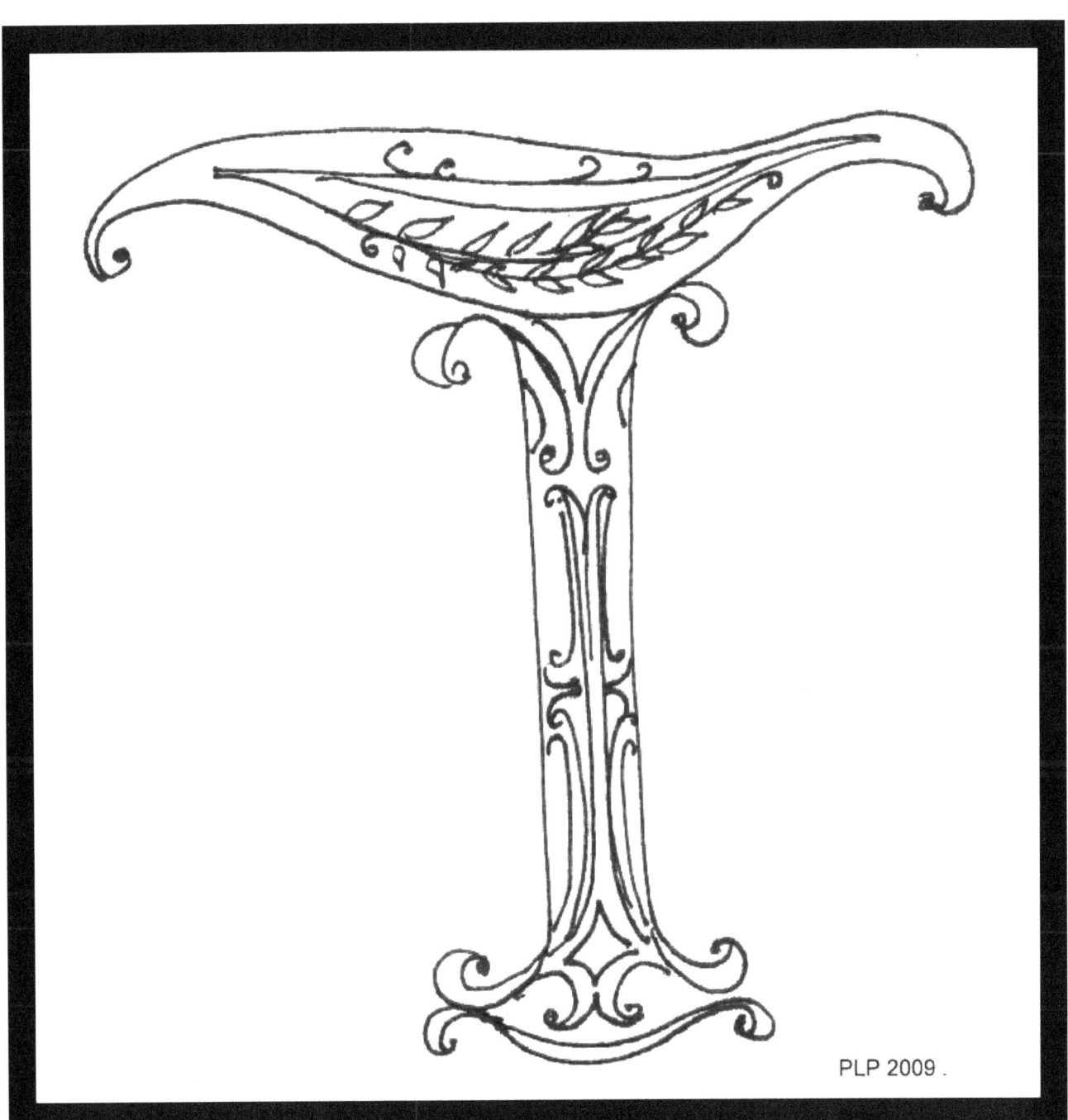

PLP 2009 .

Would you like to color this one like bandana? Leave designs white.

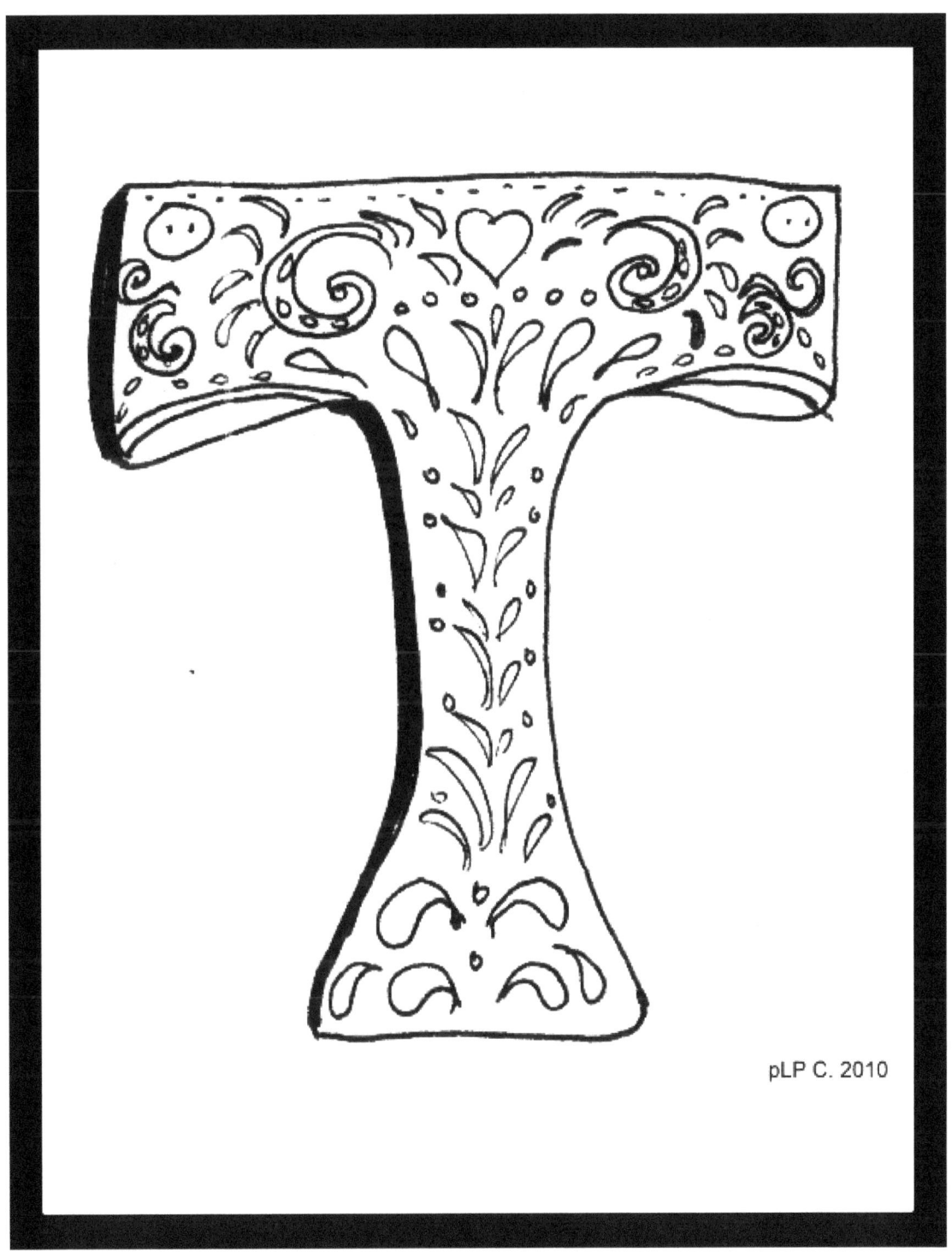

pLP C. 2010

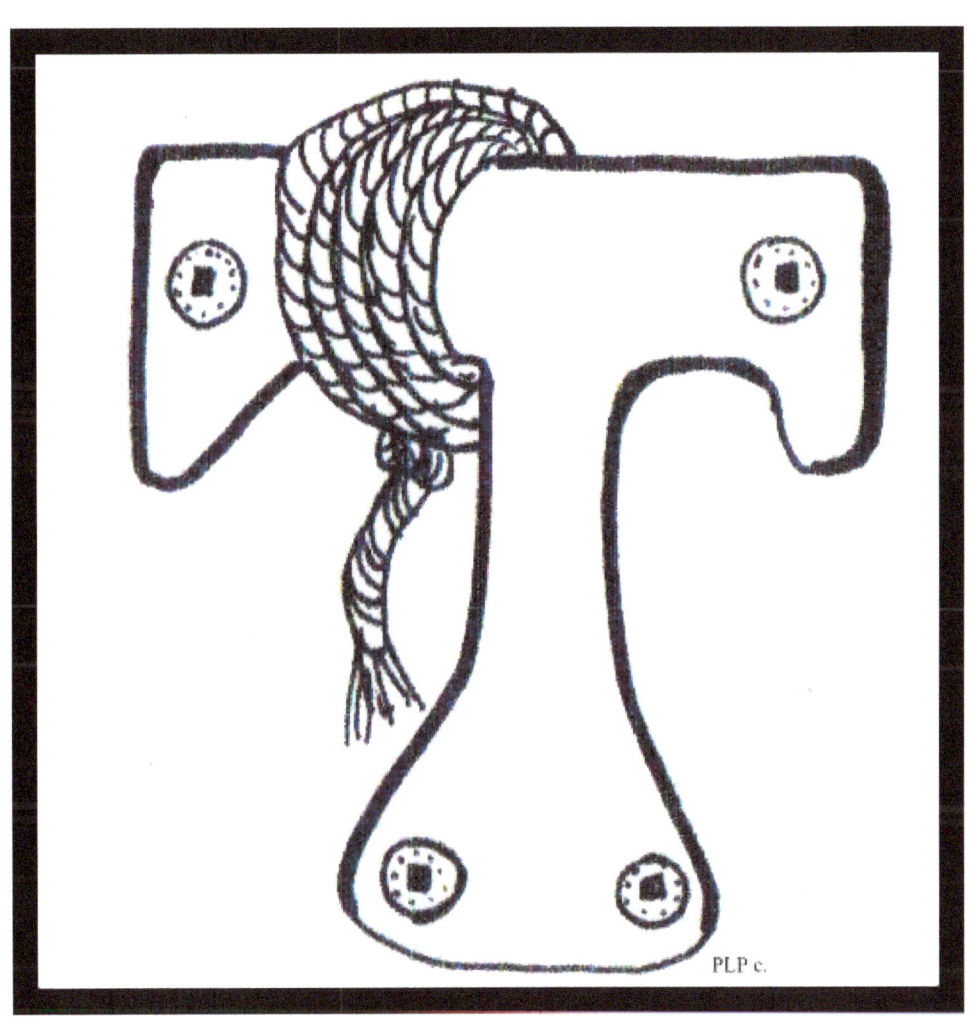

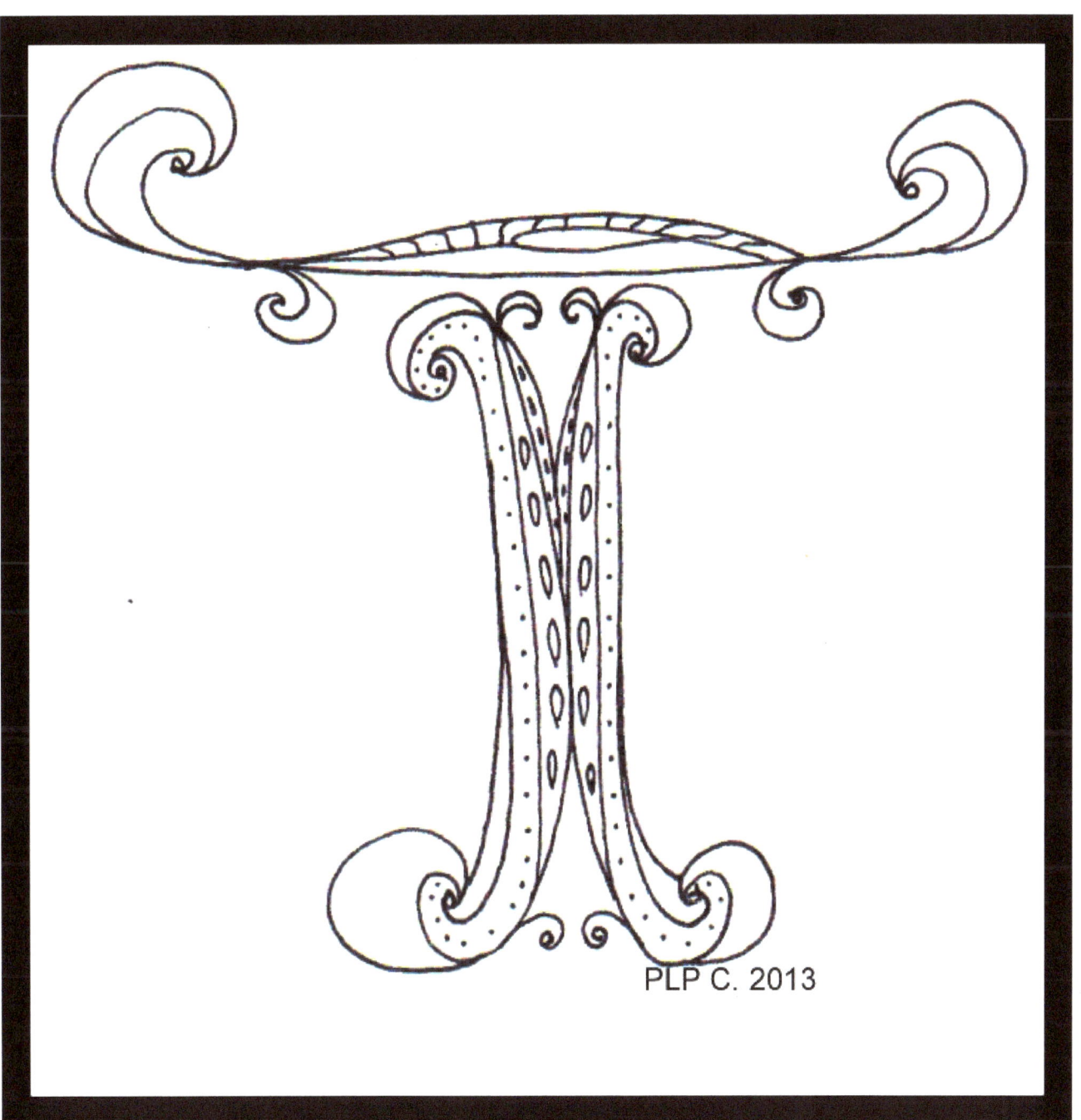

PLP C. 2013

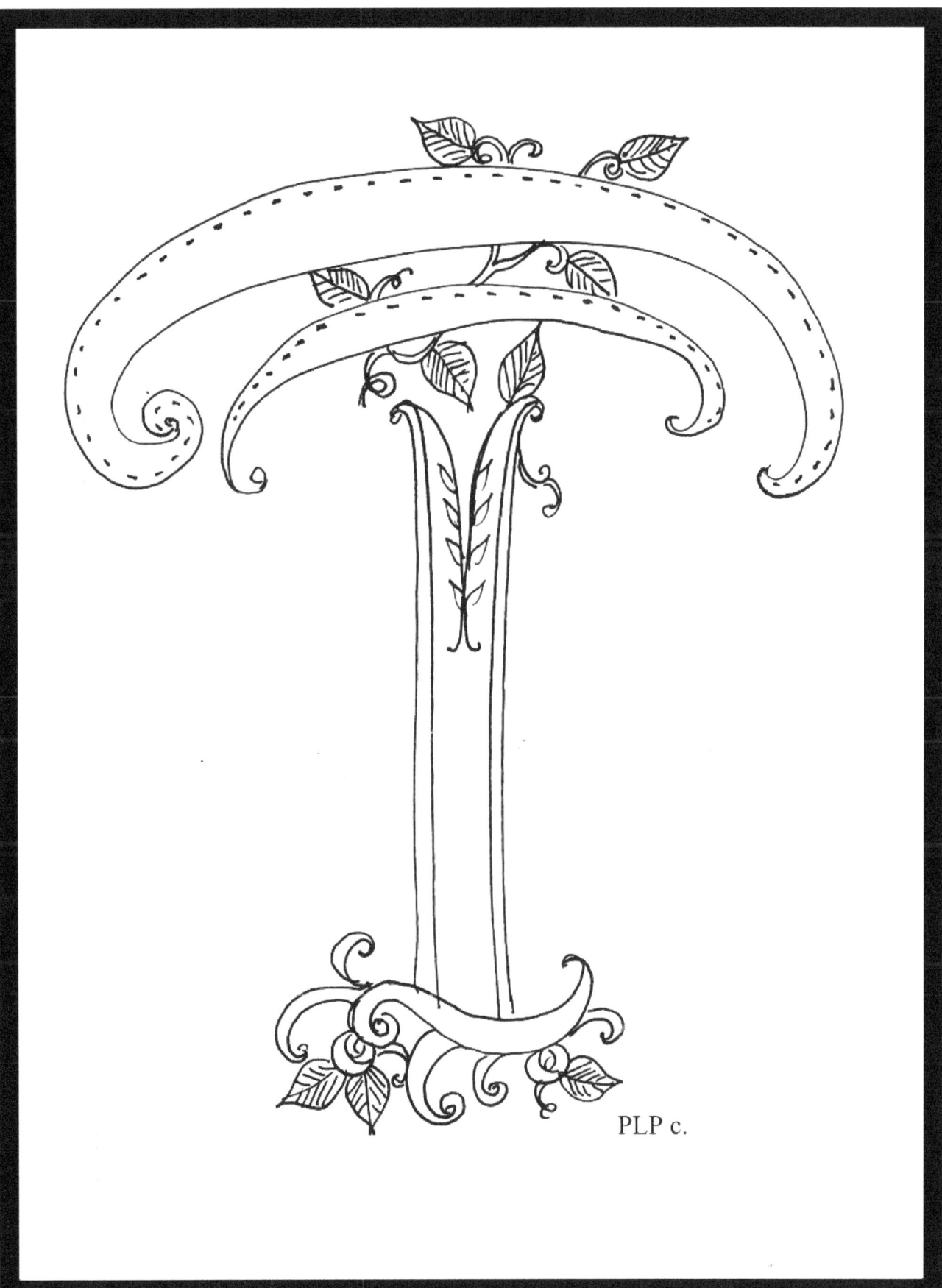

PLP c.

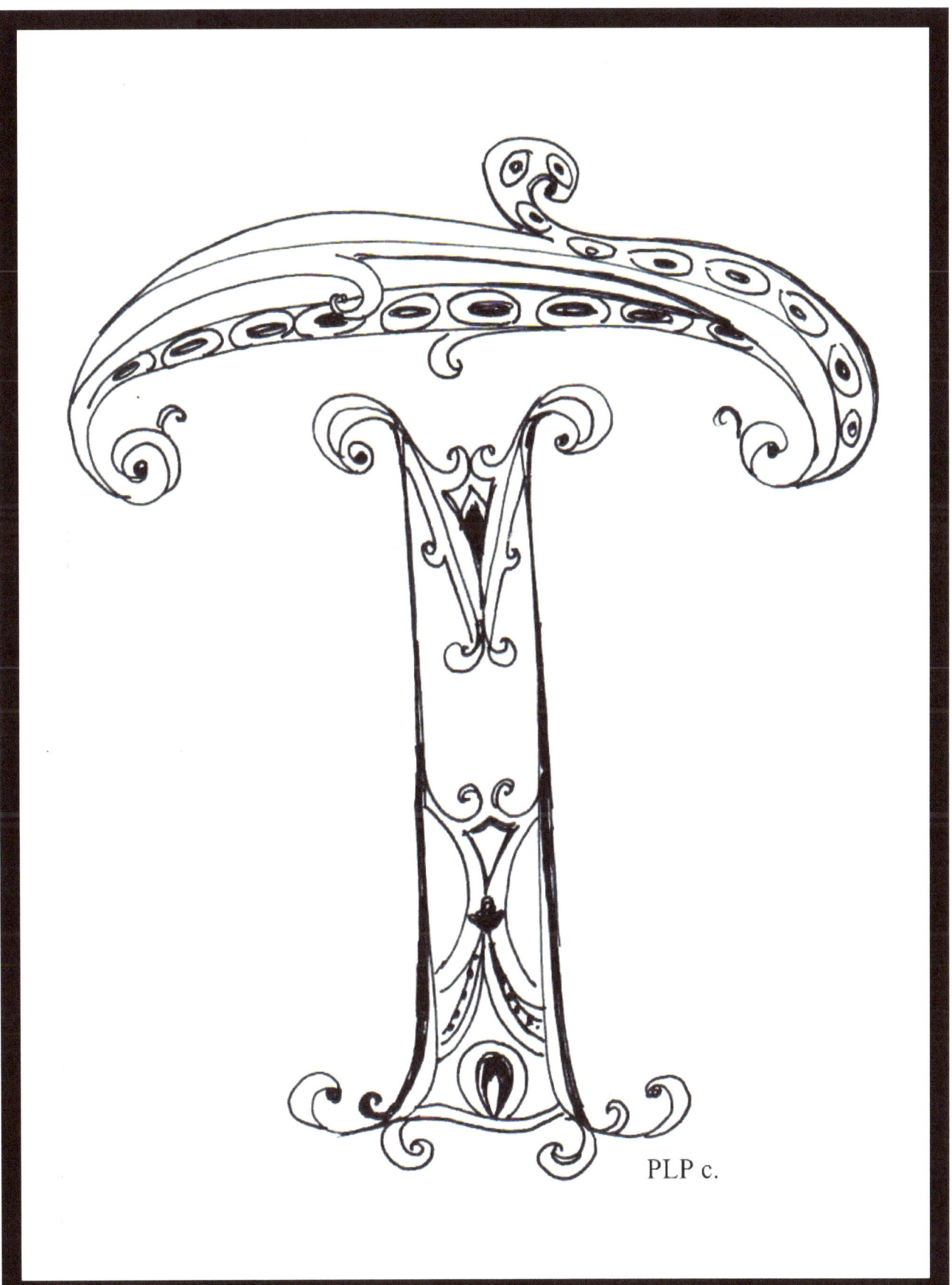

PLP c.

Look what letter "T" you can do.

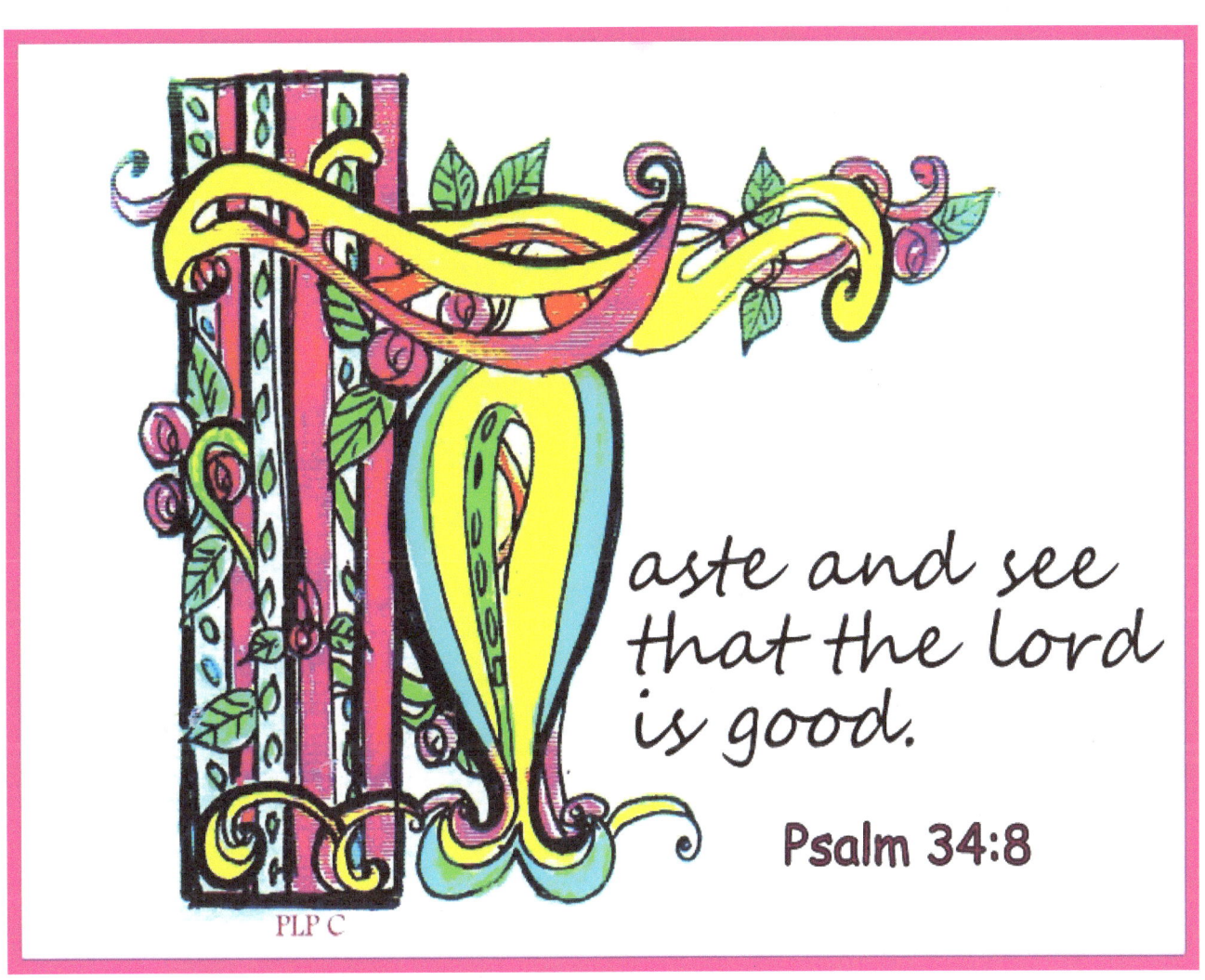

aste and see that the lord is good.

Psalm 34:8

The Letter T can pull all sorts of surprises. Did you find this T in this book?

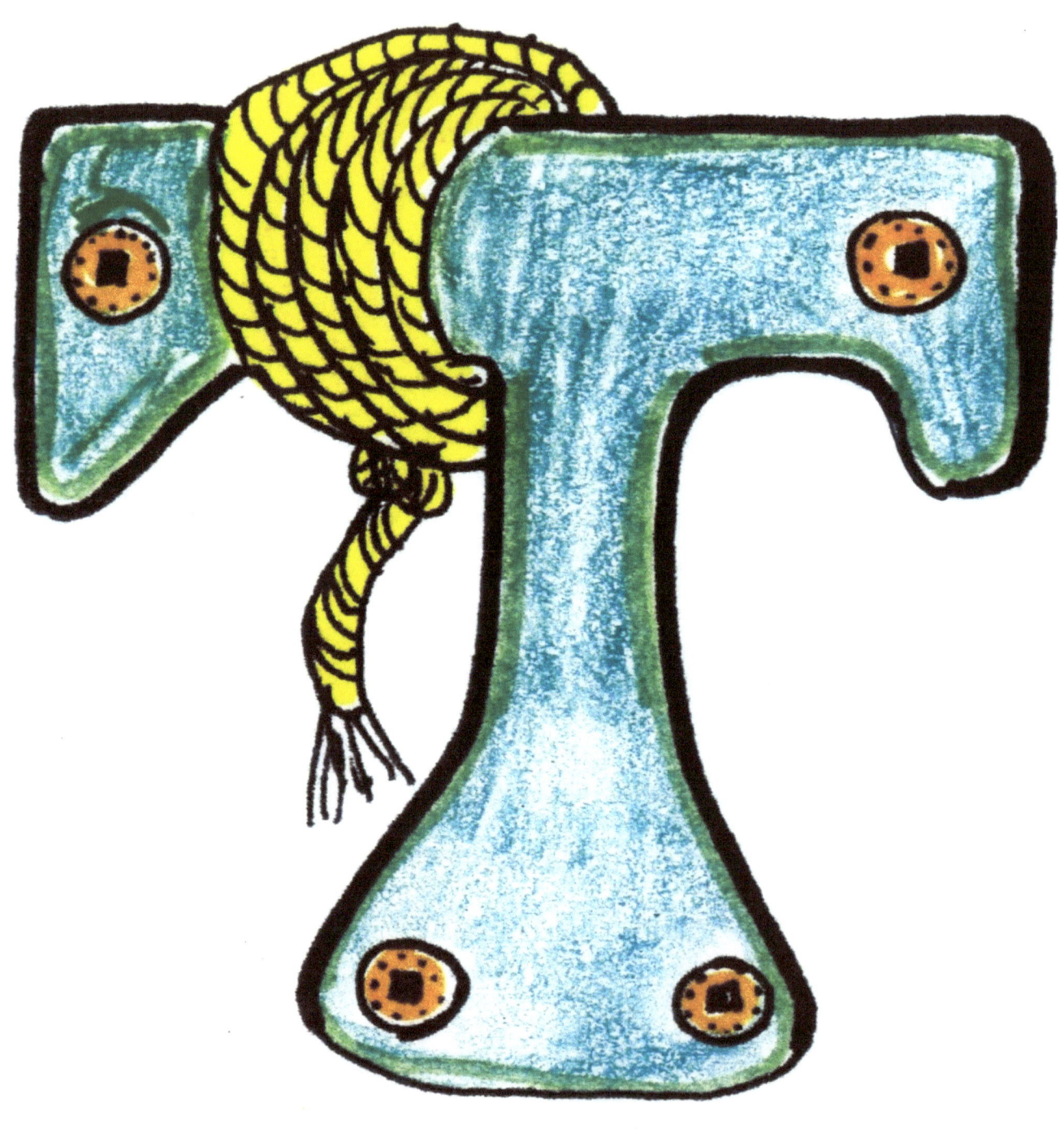

A "T" can resemble lots of fun things!

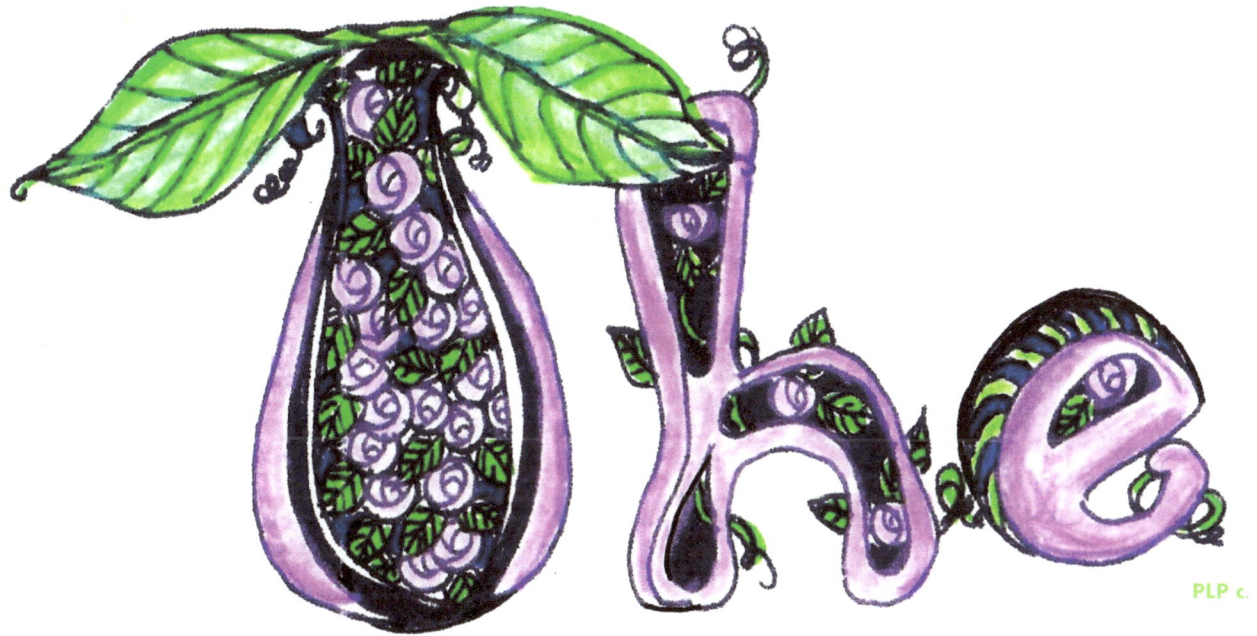

PLP c.

Letter T can be decorated to fit any occasion. Enjoy The Ts.....

Thank you for joining my T fun. Artist Peggy Louise Parrish

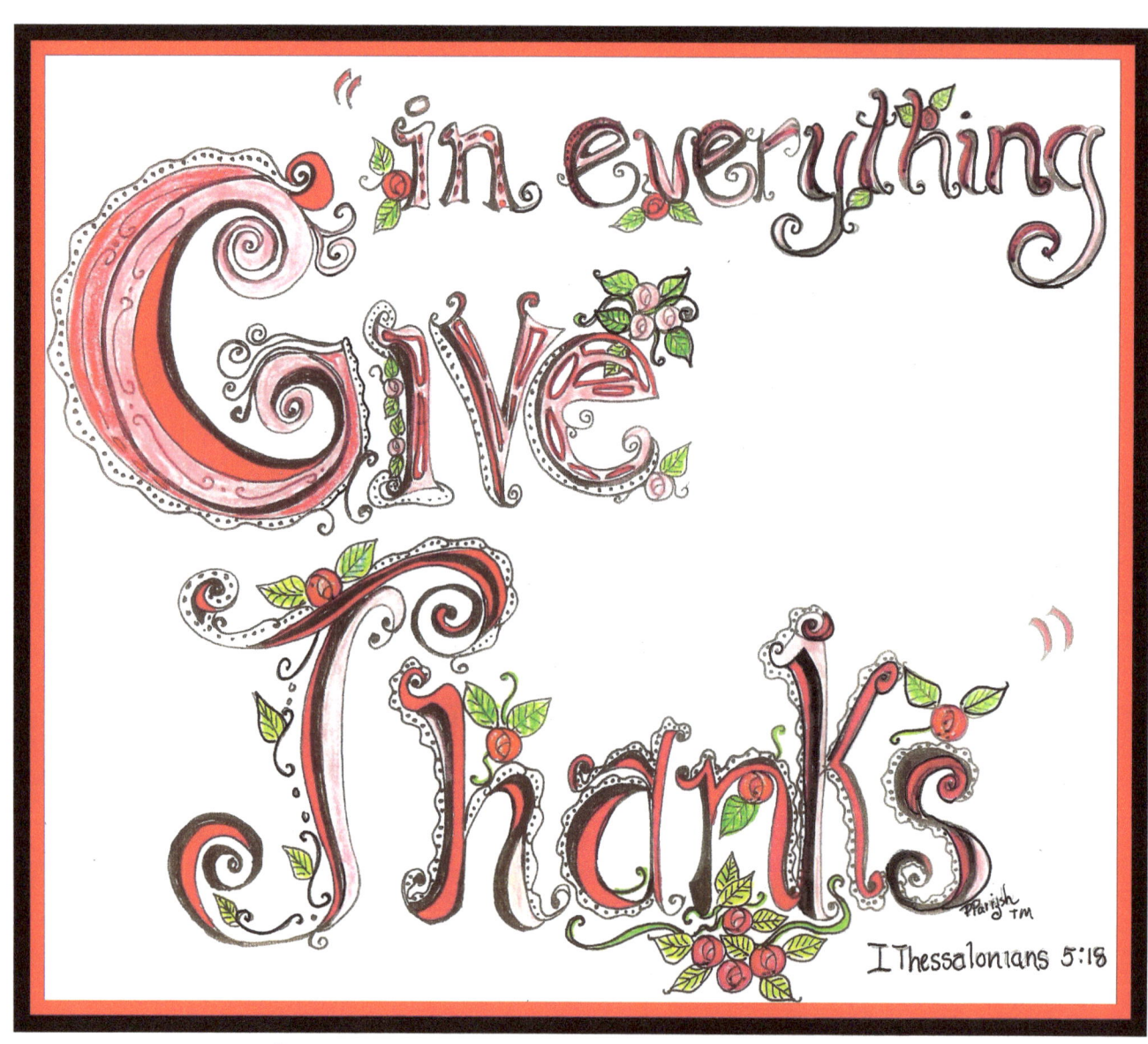

What kind of Ts can you come up with?

www.ingramcontent.com/pod-product-compliance
Lightning Source LLC
Chambersburg PA
CBHW051049180526
45172CB00002B/569